Kindergarten WORKBOOK

CANADIAN CURRICULUM PRESS

Table of Contents

by
Margaret Ann Hawkins

Editor
Lisa Penttilä

Layout & Design
Michael P. Brodey

Canadian Curriculum Press
is an imprint of Telegraph Road
12 Cranfield Road,
Toronto, Ontario, Canada
M4B 3G8

ALL RIGHTS RESERVED
ISBN: 978-177062073-5

For special bulk purchases please contact:
sales@telegraph-rd.com

For other inquiries please contact:
inquiries@telegraph-rd.com

Printed in China

CANADIAN CURRICULUM PRESS

Dear Parents,

Welcome to the Kindergarten Workbook! Its giant size makes it perfect to use on the floor with a friend or in the car on a lap.

The giant Kindergarten Workbook provides colourful activities that are ordered from easier to more challenging to keep kids absorbed and learning in an enjoyable way. It is designed to strengthen the skills your child is working on at school:

- printing letters A to Z and numbers 1 to 10
- letter recognition, letter sounds, rhyming, and an introduction to word recognition and printing simple words
- counting, number recognition, sorting, more and less
- colours, patterns, and measuring
- weeks, months, and seasons

Along the way, children build important fine motor skills plus left-to-right and top-to-bottom focus.

You can support your child's learning by making sure he or she understands the instructions, praising effort, and finishing each session when your child shows signs of tiring. Of course, talking about letters and numbers, noticing patterns, and playing rhyming games are things you can do together at the grocery store, in the car, or wherever your day takes you. Having fun while doing these things together creates a positive atmosphere around learning.

The Kindergarten Workbook helps children experience success with new challenges. The skills they learning now create the founda... success in the primary grades and beyond!

Sincerely,

Margaret Ann Hawkins

Margaret Ann Hawkins, B.A., B. Ed.

All About Me

This is me!

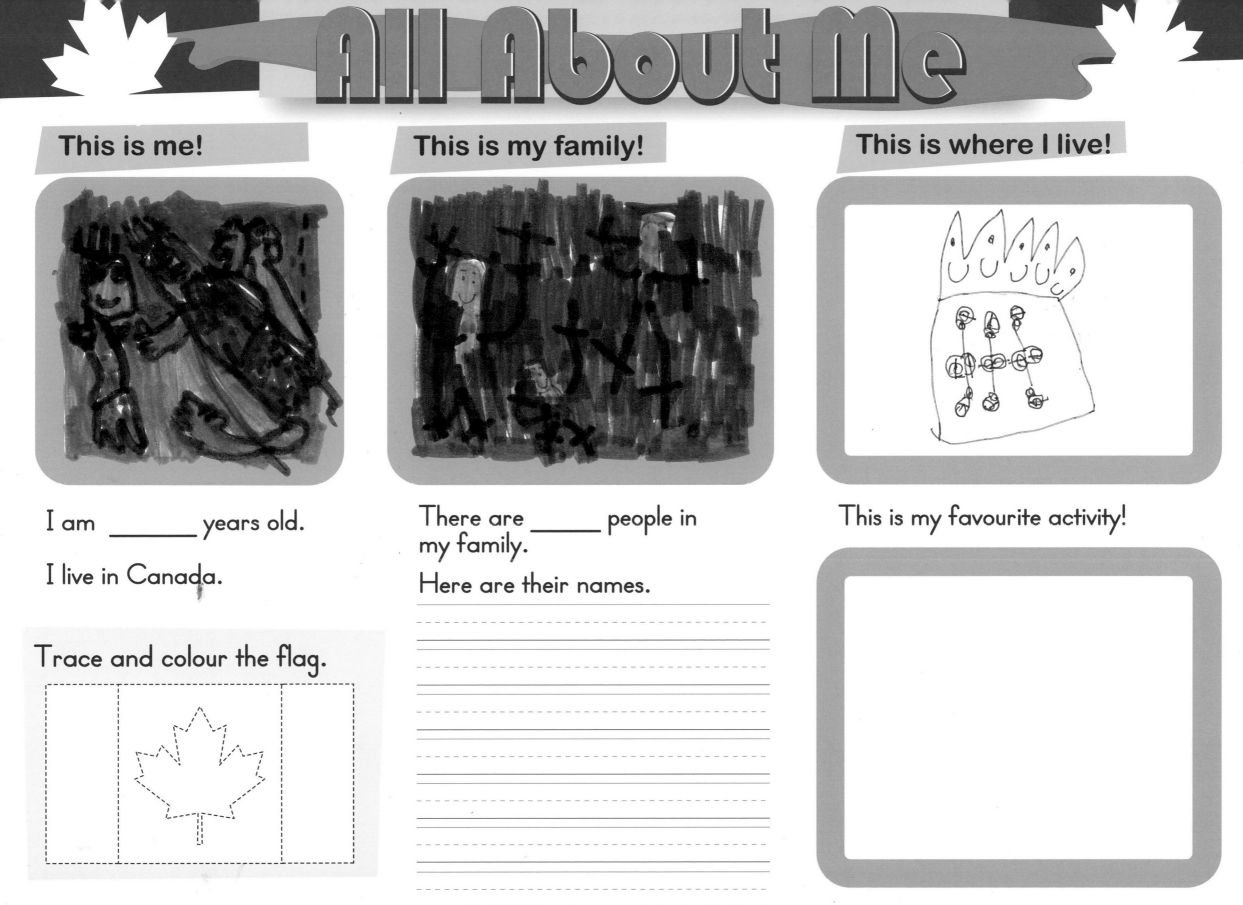

I am _____ years old.

I live in Canada.

Trace and colour the flag.

This is my family!

There are _____ people in my family.

Here are their names.

_____

_____

_____

_____

_____

_____

_____

_____

_____

_____

_____

This is where I live!

This is my favourite activity!

I Know My Colours!

Trace the colour words.

red   blue   orange   green

yellow   brown   purple   black

Colour the paint brushes.

| red | blue | yellow | orange | green | black | purple | brown |

3

Match the picture to the colour word.
One is done.

yellow

brown

purple

black

blue

green

orange

red

Super Sorting

Sort the fruit. Circle the ones that are different.

Sort the balloons.
Colour the small balloons with your favourite colour. Put an X on the big balloons.

Look at each picture.
Draw what is missing.

Draw an X on the one that doesn't belong.

Aa

Bb

Learning About Letters

Trace and print A and a. Say the letter sound.

A A A A A A A A A

A

a a a a a a a a a a

a

Trace and print B and b. Say the letter sound.

B B B B B B B B B

B

b b b b b b b b b b

b

Circle things that start with a.

Circle things that start with b.

Start at the pencil and follow the a b path to the finish.

Finish

5

Learning About Letters

Trace and print C and c. Say the letter sound.

C C C C C C C C

c

c c c c c c c c c c

Trace and print D and d. Say the letter sound.

D D D D D D D D D

D

d d d d d d d d d d

d

Circle things that start with c.

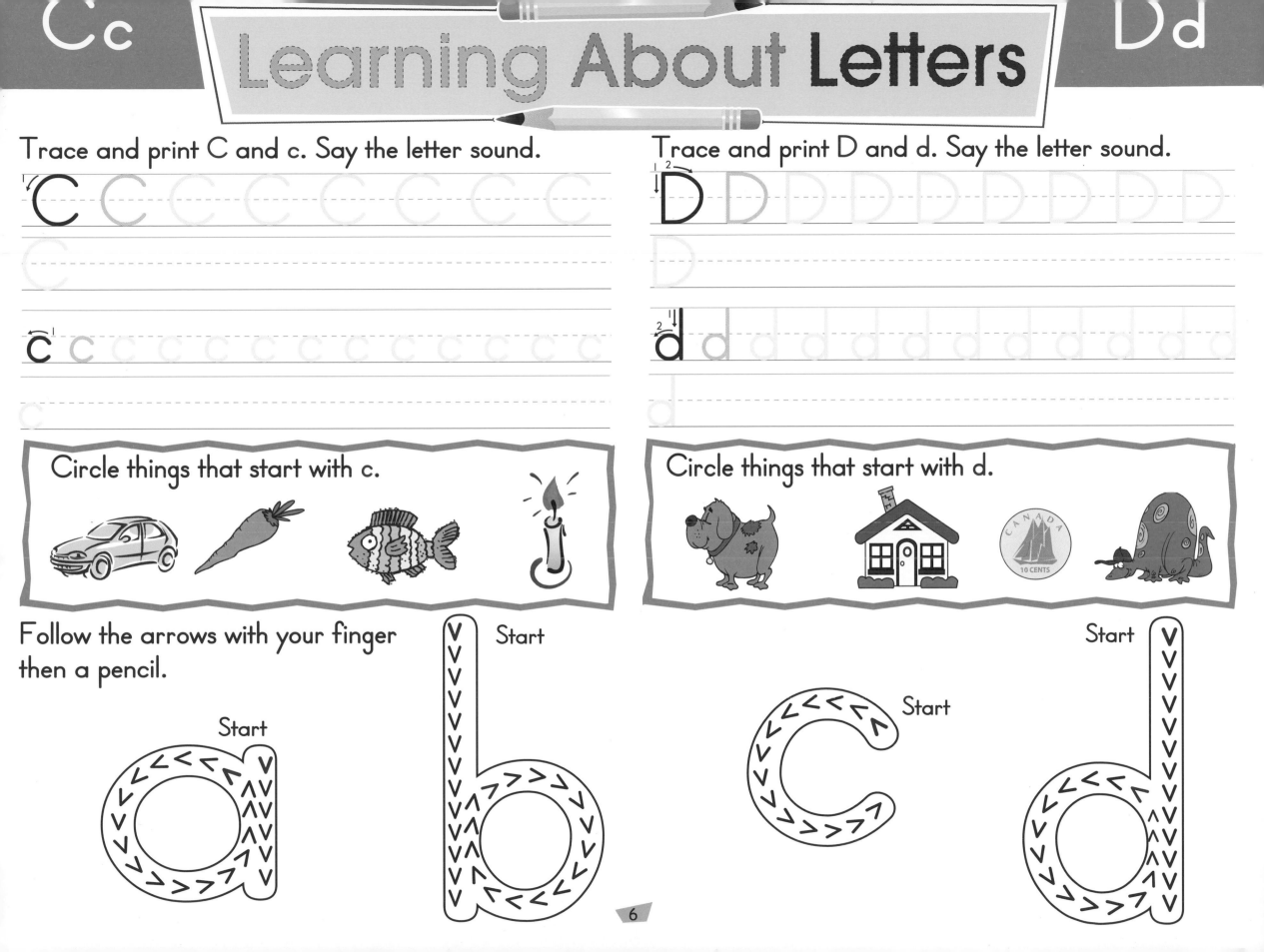

Circle things that start with d.

Follow the arrows with your finger then a pencil.

Start

Start

Start

Start

Learning About Letters

Trace and print E and e. Say the letter sound.

Trace and print F and f. Say the letter sound.

E

e

F

f

Colour things that start with e.

Colour things that start with f.

Learning About Letters

Trace and print G and g. Say the letter sound.

G G G G G G G G G

G

g g g g g g g g g g g

g

Trace and print H and h. Say the letter sound.

H H H H H H H H H

H

h h h h h h h h h h h

h

Follow the arrows with your finger then a pencil.

e   Start

Start f

g   Start h

Colour things blue that start with g.
Colour things green that start with h.

8

Learning About Letters

Trace and print I and i. Say the letter sound.

Trace and print J and j. Say the letter sound.

Circle things that start with i.

Circle things that start with j.

Learning About Letters

Trace and print K and k. Say the letter sound.

K K K K K K K K K

K

k k k k k k k k k k

k

Trace and print L and l. Say the letter sound.

L L L L L L L L L L L

l l l l l l l l l l l l

Follow the arrows with your finger then a pencil.

Start

Start

Start

Start

i j k l

Circle things that start with k.

Circle things that start with l.

Learning About Letters

Trace and print M and m. Say the letter sound.

M M M M M M M M

M

m m m m m m m m

m

Trace and print N and n. Say the letter sound.

N N N N N N N N

N

n n n n n n n n

n

Draw 2 things that start with m.

Draw 2 things that start with n.

Learning About Letters

Trace and print O and o. Say the letter sound.

O O O O O O O O O O O

O

o o o o o o o o o o o

o

Trace and print P and p. Say the letter sound.

P P P P P P P P P P P P

P

p p p p p p p p p p p p

p

Follow the arrows with your finger then a pencil.

Start

m

Start

n

Colour things that start with o.

Circle and colour things that start with p.

Start

o

Start

p

Learning About Letters

Trace and print Q and q. Say the letter sound.

Q Q Q Q Q Q Q Q Q

Q

q q q q q q q q q q

q

Trace and print R and r. Say the letter sound.

R R R R R R R R R R

R

r r r r r r r r r r

r

Follow the q's to get to the "R".

13

Learning About Letters

Trace and print S and s. Say the letter sound.

S S S S S S S S S S

S

s s s s s s s s s s

s

Trace and print T and t. Say the letter sound.

T T T T T T T T T

T

t t t t t t t t t t

t

Follow the arrows with your finger then a pencil.

Start

q

Start

r

Start

t

Start

s

Draw 2 things that start with s.

Colour 3 things that start with t.

Learning About Letters

Trace and print U and u. Say the letter sound.

Trace and print V and v. Say the letter sound.

Put a ✔ on things that start with u.

UP

Put a ✔ on things that start with v.

♪ Violin Music Maze

Follow the alphabet through the violin to find the letter v.

Start

a k l o p
b p m n r q
  j   s
  i h g t   v Exit
c e   u
d f

violin

Learning About Letters

Trace and print W and w. Say the letter sound.

W

W

w

W

Trace and print X and x. Say the letter sound.

X

X

x

X

Follow the arrows with your finger then a pencil.

Start

U

Start

V

Start

W

Start

X

Colour things that start with w.

Colour things that start or end with x.

6

Learning About Letters

Trace and print Y and y. Say the letter sound.

Y Y Y Y Y Y Y Y Y

y Y Y Y Y Y Y Y Y

Trace and print Z and z. Say the letter sound.

Z Z Z Z Z Z Z Z Z

z Z Z Z Z Z Z Z Z

Follow the arrows with your finger then a pencil.

Start

Colour things that start with y.

Circle things that start with z.

Start

I Know All My Letters!

a b c d e f g h i j k l m n o p q r s t u v w x y z

Draw a line from the picture to the letter it starts with. The first one is done for you.

Draw a line from the letter to the picture that starts with that sound. The first one is done for you.

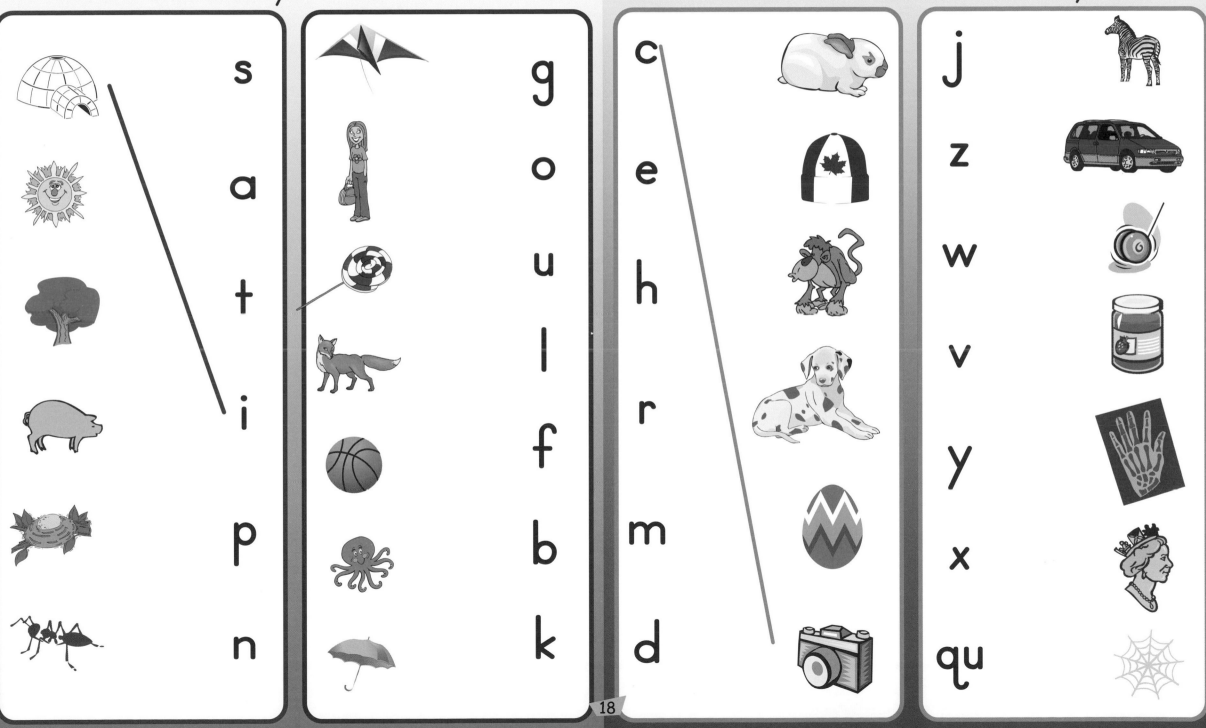

Hooray for Patterns!

A pattern repeats over and over.
Look at this pattern.
Say the name of the shapes.

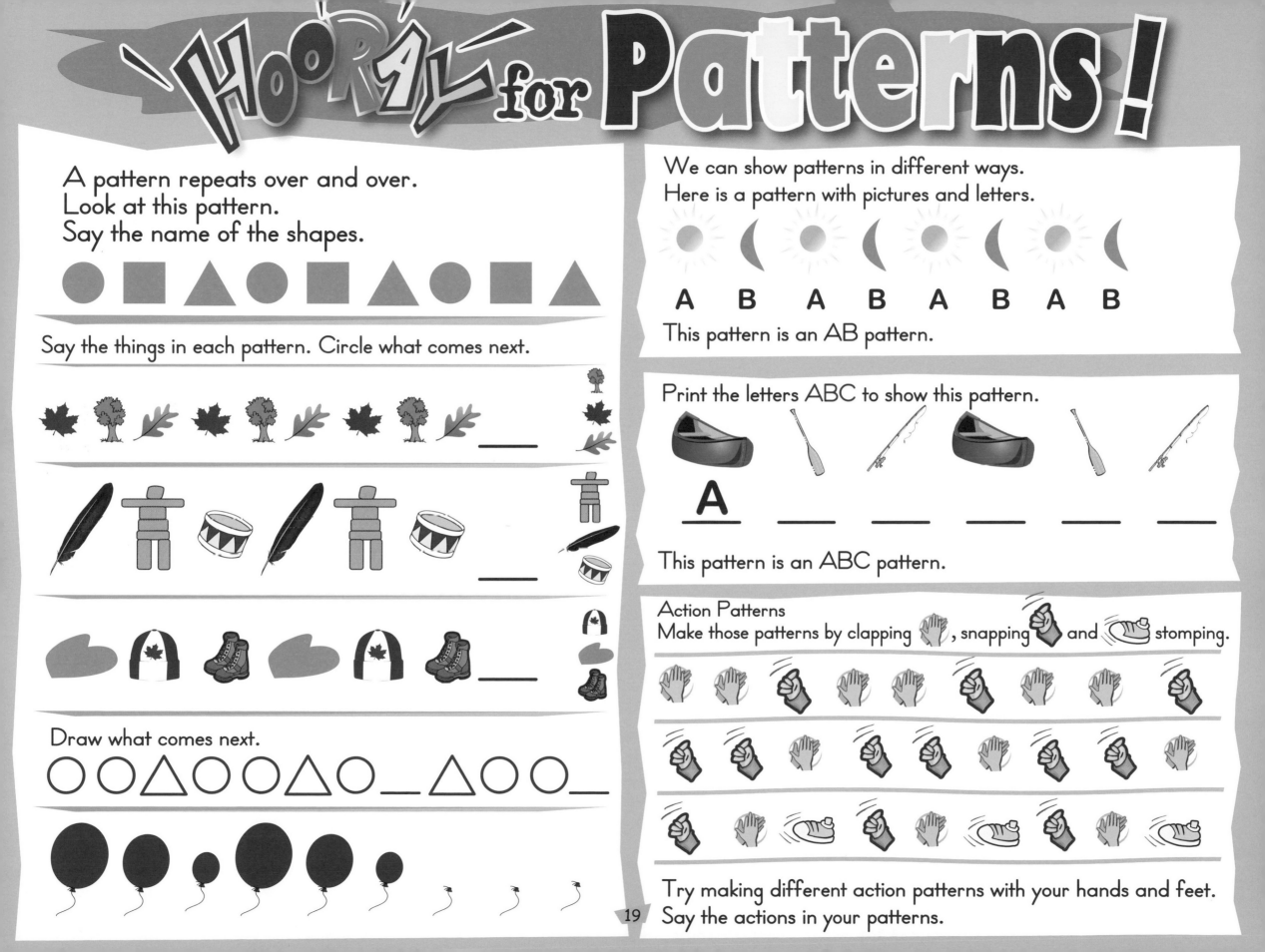

Say the things in each pattern. Circle what comes next.

Draw what comes next.

We can show patterns in different ways.
Here is a pattern with pictures and letters.

A B A B A B A B

This pattern is an AB pattern.

Print the letters ABC to show this pattern.

A _ _ _ _ _ _

This pattern is an ABC pattern.

Action Patterns
Make those patterns by clapping, snapping and stomping.

Try making different action patterns with your hands and feet.
Say the actions in your patterns.

Colour and Create Patterns

Use red R yellow Y and blue B to continue the pattern.
Say the colours.

R Y B ___ ___ ___ ___ ___ ___ ___

R R R B B B ___ ___ ___ ___ ___ ___

Colour the pictures to make patterns. Tell what patterns you made.

Use ● ▲ ■ to make your own pattern. Tell what pattern you made.

1 one

2 two

Trace and print the number 1.

one

Trace and print the number 2.

two

Follow the path to the lake.

Start

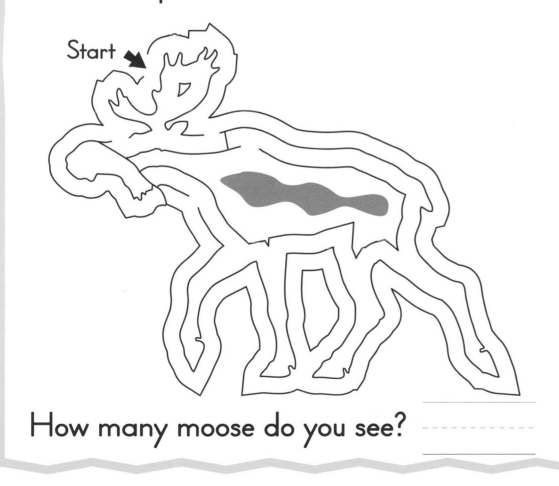

How many moose do you see? _____

Count the fish.

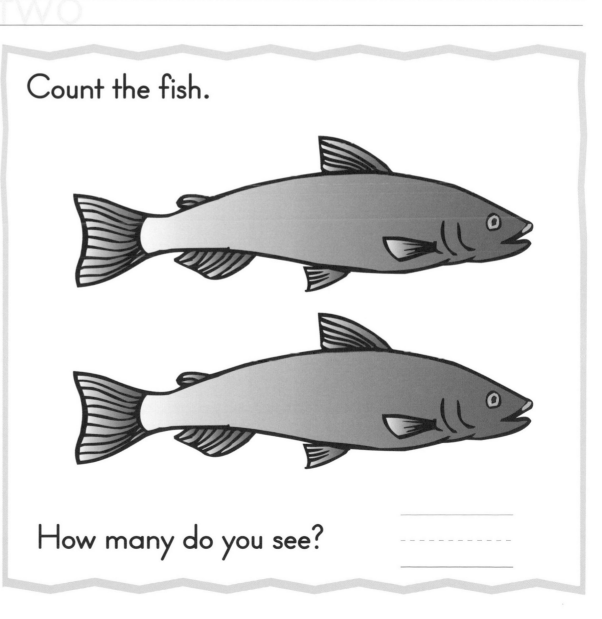

How many do you see? _____

Trace and print the number 3.

3 3 3 3 3 3 3 3 3 3

three

Colour the beavers.

How many do you see? _____

Trace and print the number 4.

4 4 4 4 4 4 4 4 4

four

Count the Canada geese.

How many do you see? _____

Trace and print the number 5.

5 5 5 5 5 5 5 5 5 5 5 5

5

five

Trace and print the number 6.

6 6 6 6 6 6 6 6 6 6 6

6

six

Colour the whales.

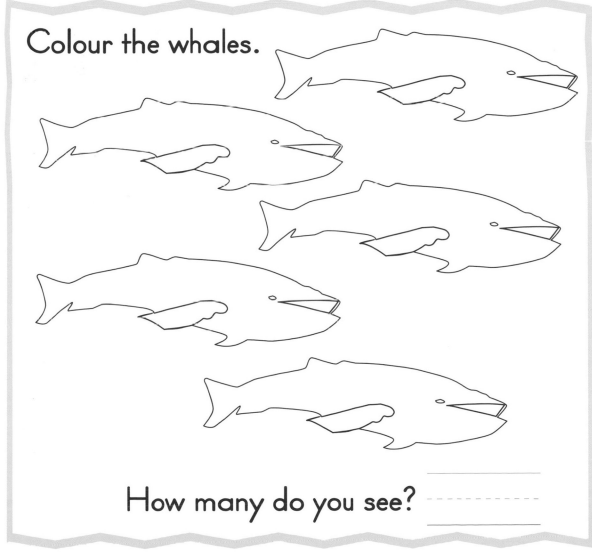

How many do you see? _____

Count the bears.

How many do you see? _____

Trace and print the number 7.

7 7 7 7 7 7 7 7 7 7

seven

Trace and print the number 8.

8 8 8 8 8 8 8 8 8 8 8

eight

Colour the wolves.

How many do you see? _____

Count the racoons.

How many do you see? _____

Trace and print the number 9.

9 q q q q q q q q q

9

nine

Trace and print the number 10.

10 10 10 10 10 10 10

10

ten

Colour the deer.

How many do you see? _____

Count the loons.

How many do you see? _____

Hooray for Counting!

How many?
Circle the number.

(rabbit) 1　2　3	(balloons) 2　3　4
(ducks) 3　4　5	(fish) 1　2　3
(crayons) 2　3　4	(party hats) 3　4　5
(hats) 1　2　3	(loons) 3　4　5
(cakes) 3　4　5	(pumpkins) 1　2　3

Look at the number.
Draw a line to the matching picture.

1

2

3

4

5

Hooray for Counting!

How many? Circle the number.

(globes) 6 7 8	(ghosts) 7 8 9
(gifts) 7 8 9	(sunglasses) 8 9 10
(hearts) 8 9 10	(lions) 4 5 6
(drums) 6 7 8	(candy) 8 9 10
(hippos) 8 9 10	(apples) 6 7 8

Look at the number. Draw a line to the matching picture.

6

7

8

9

10

(snowflakes)

(stars)

(suns)

(maple leaves)

(eggs)

Count. Circle the group that has more.

Count. Circle the group that has less.

Follow the instructions to finish each picture.

Draw 3 fish in the fish bowl.

Draw 5 apples on the tree.

Draw 6 cookies on the plate.

Draw 4 balloons for the girl.

Connect the dots from 1 to 10.

Start

10 9

8

7

2

3 4

6

5

Days, Months and Seasons

Days of the week

There are 7 days in the week.
Can you say the names?

Sunday
Monday
Tuesday
Wednesday
Thursday
Friday
Saturday

Yesterday was _____

Today is _____

Tomorrow will be _____

My favourite day of the week is

_____

There are four seasons in a year. Put a number to tell which one comes next. Start at spring.

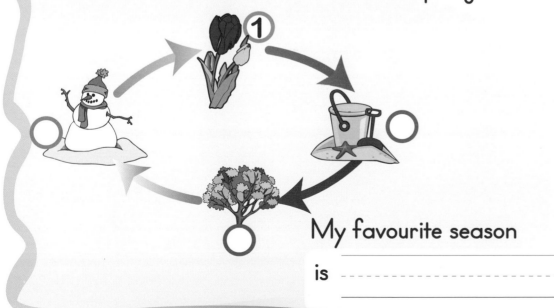

①

My favourite season

is _____

Months of the year

There are 12 months in the year.
Can you say the names?

January
February
March
April
May
June

July
August
September
October
November
December

My birthday is in _____

What is the weather? Draw a line from the weather to the clothes you would need.

Trace each shape with your finger. Say its name.

circle   square   triangle   rectangle

Colour the shapes that belong in each family.

circle family

square family

triangle family

rectangle family

Look at the picture. Count the shapes.

How many ○ ? _____

How many ◻ ? _____

How many ▭ ? _____

How many △ ? _____

Trace and draw:

square

triangle

circle

rectangle

30

3-D Shapes

cube   sphere   cylinder   cone   rectangular prism

Colour the sphere ⬤ shapes red.

Colour the cube ▨ shapes blue.

Colour the cylinder ▢ shapes green.

Colour the cone 🔺 shapes orange.

Colour the rectangular prism ▭ shapes purple.

Cereal Shapes

Look for things at home that have these shapes. Draw what you find.

✔ or X

☐

☐

☐

☐

☐

Put a ✔ beside the shape you found the most of.

31 Put an **X** beside the shape you found the least of.

It's Time to Measure

Cut a piece of string as long as your arm.
Find something longer than the string.
Find something the same length as the string.
Find something shorter than the string.

Draw what you found.

Longer than the string	Same length as the string	Shorter than the string

Count the squares.
Write the number of squares tall each house is.

_____ squares tall   _____ squares tall   _____ squares tall

Heavy or Light?

Colour heavy things green.
Colour light things red.

Which holds more?

Circle the one that holds more.
Make an X on the one that holds less.

32

Let's Make Words!

Look at the pictures. Say the words. Print the letters you hear.

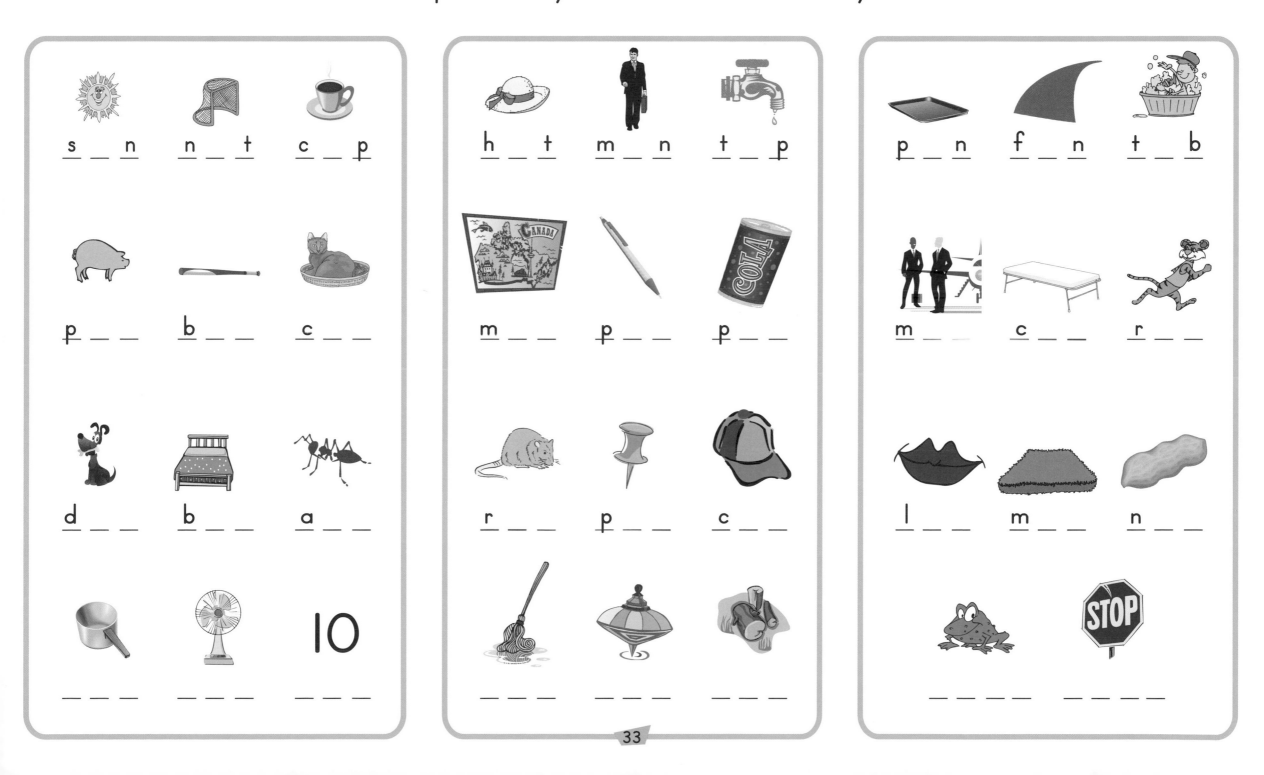

s _ n   n _ t   c _ p

p _ _   b _ _   c _ _

d _ _   b _ _   a _ _

_ _ _   _ _ _   _ _ _

h _ t   m _ n   t _ p

m _ _ _   p _ _   p _ _

r _ _   p _ _   c _ _

_ _ _   _ _ _   _ _ _

p _ n   f _ n   t _ b

m _ _   c _ _   r _ _

l _ _   m _ _   n _ _

_ _ _   _ _ _

Rhyme Time!

Rhyming words start with different sounds and end with the same sound. Draw a line to each rhyming pair. One is done for you.

hat — cat
mouse
tree
pie
fan
log
pen
jar

house
three 3
pan
frog
cat
tie
car
ten 10

Read the words from the rhyming word families.

at	ap	en
sat	cap	den
cat	map	pen
hat	lap	men
mat	nap	hen
rat	tap	ten
pat	gap	

an	et	ut
can	pet	but
man	get	cut
fan	wet	hut
tan	met	nut
ran	let	gut
van	yet	rut

in	ot	it
pin	dot	hit
tin	got	pit
win	hot	sit
fin	not	
	pot	
	lot	

Make rhyming words by adding the letter on the left to the pair of letters on the right. Say each word.

p ——▶ __op
t ——▶ __op
m ——▶ __op

m ——▶ __et
g ——▶ __et
w ——▶ __et

r ——▶ __ip
t ——▶ __ip
s ——▶ __ip

d ——▶ __og
l ——▶ __og
h ——▶ __og

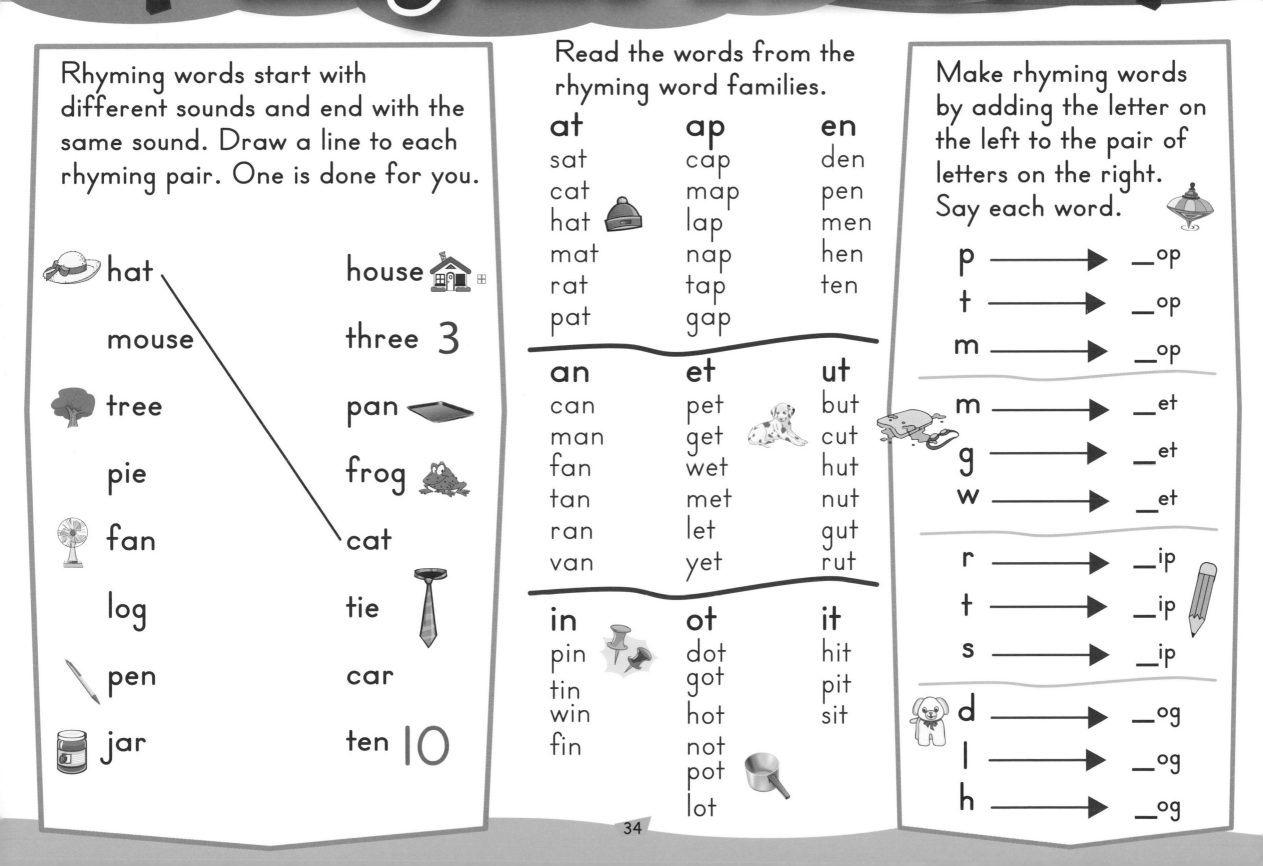

34

What Comes Next?

Draw the missing picture.

Draw the missing picture.

Look at the pictures below.

Tell what is happening in each story. Use numbers 1 2 3 4   to put pictures in the correct order.

Making a birthday cake:

○   ○   ○   ○

Making eggs for breakfast:

○   ○   ○   ○

Making a snowman:

○

○

Making toast:

○   ○   ○   ○

I Know My Colours - Page 3

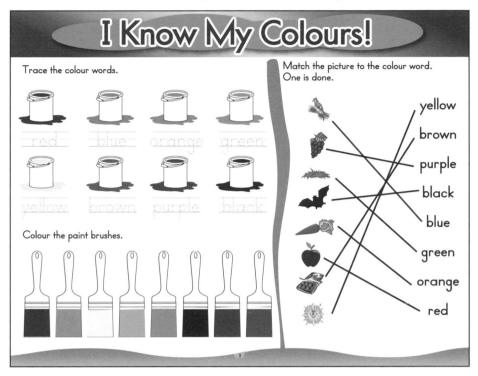

I Know All My Letters - Page 18

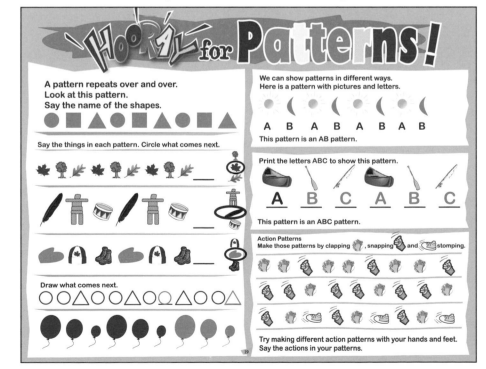

Super Sorting - Page 4

Hooray for Patterns - Page 19

Answers

Colour and Create Patterns - Page 20

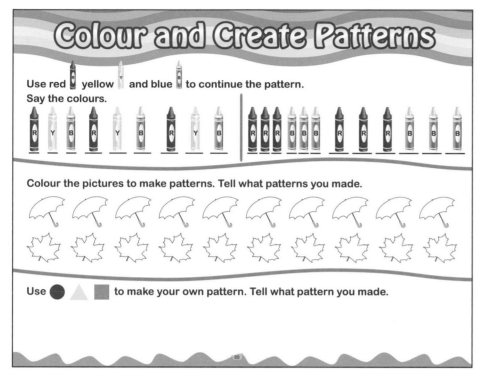

Hooray for Counting 6 -10 - Page 27

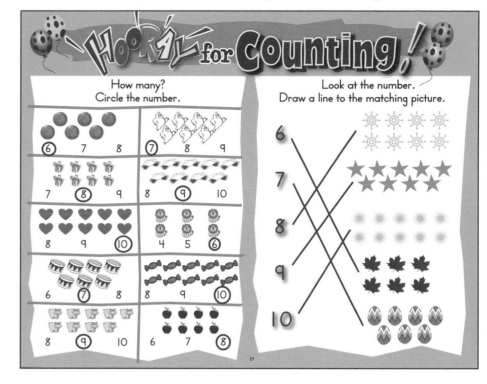

Hooray for Counting 1-5 - Page 26

I Can Count - Page 28

Days, Months and Years – Page 29

3-D Shapes - Page 31

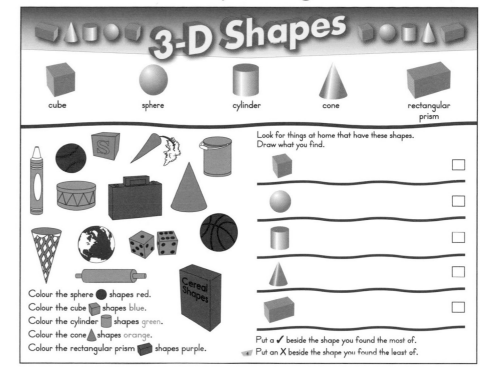

2-D Shapes - Page 30

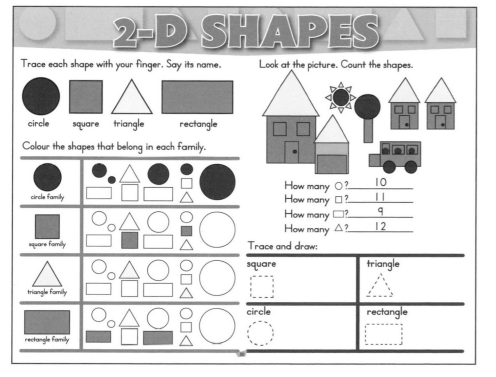

How many ○? 10
How many □? 11
How many ▭? 9
How many △? 12

It's Time to Measure - Page 32

4 squares tall
6 squares tall
8 squares tall